Legends of JOURNEYS

by Olga Norris

illustrated by Bryna Waldman

CAMBRIDGE UNIVERSITY PRESS

Cambridge
New York   New Rochelle
Melbourne   Sydney

Other legends books from Cambridge

Legends of the Animal World by Rosalind Kerven

Legends of Earth, Air, Fire and Water by Eric and Tessa Hadley

Legends of the Sun and Moon by Eric and Tessa Hadley

The Seven Wonders of the World by Kenneth McLeish

The Shining Stars by Ghislaine Vautier and Kenneth McLeish

The Way of the Stars by Ghislaine Vautier and Kenneth McLeish

Published by the Press Syndicate of the University of Cambridge
The Pitt Building, Trumpington Street, Cambridge CB2 1RP
32 East 57th Street, New York, NY 10022, USA
10 Stamford Road, Oakleigh, Melbourne 3166, Australia

First published 1988

Printed in Hong Kong by Wing King Tong

British Library cataloguing in publication data
Norris, Olga
    Legends of journeys.
    I. Title II. Waldman, Bryna
    823′.914[J]   PZ7

Library of Congress Cataloguing in Publication Data
Norris, Olga, 1948–
    Legends of journeys.
    Summary: A collection of traditional tales about travel from
various parts of the world.
    1. Voyages and travel – Folklore – Juvenile literature. 2. Tales.
[1. Voyages and travels – Folklore. 2. Folklore] I. Waldman,
Bryna, ill.
II. Title.
PZ8.1.N7925Le 1987   398.2′7 [E]   86-2638

ISBN 0 521 32181 6

DS

CONTENTS

About the stories

ABOUT THE STORIES

All the stories in this book are tales that old people have told their young, generation after generation. Every generation of old folk makes small changes to the stories, here and there, to make them fit the situation of the time. In many parts of the world this is how all knowledge is handed on. There is a saying that 'when an old African dies a whole library is burnt'. Today we are lucky because we have books in which we can read all these stories without having to spend a lifetime travelling round the world to meet the storytellers; but this also means that we have to think harder about the stories and try to imagine what they might mean to the people in the places they come from.

The legends in this book are about journeys. Journeys are important to all of us – whether they are short journeys that we make every day, such as going to school, or longer journeys, such as visiting relatives, or special journeys made only once in a lifetime.

There are always three main parts to a journey: the beginning, the middle, and the end. The beginning is where the journey starts, and why the journey is being made. The middle is the journey itself, the way there and what happens on that way. The end is the arrival at the destination. Often the most interesting part of a journey is the middle.

Travelling can be great fun, and many people go on journeys simply to enjoy this, rather than wanting to reach a special end. In fact the end can be the same place as the beginning – back home. Sometimes you may decide to set out for one particular place but the destination is not quite what you expected as in Aziz's

search for *The City of Ultimate Happiness and Beauty*.

Some journeys have a different kind of end: when the traveller is setting out to look for something, or to find something out. In these cases the end of a journey is not a particular place, but is instead the discovery of whatever the traveller wanted to know or to find. This happens to the young hunter in *A Visit to the Spirits of Mount Katahdin*.

Not all journeys are voluntary. It is not always the travellers who decide where they will be going or what they will be looking for. Sometimes people are forced to leave the place where they live. This may be because of a natural disaster – such as a flood or an earthquake – or because something dreadful has happened within their own society. The peaceful Pai tribe are forced to leave their homes in the North American Indian story, *Scatter Throughout the Land*.

Another kind of journey that we all go on is the journey of life. We all start by being born, then we all live our different lives until, in the end, we die. That is what is meant by the expression 'life's great journey'. Often the stories told by the old folk are to help the young ones make the right decisions about how to live their lives, such as the African tale, *The Other Side of the Hills*.

When you have read the legends in this book, think about what kind of journey each story is. Then tell one of the stories to someone younger than you who has not read them. Try changing the story here and there to make the meaning fit today's world, just as the old folk have handed on these stories from generation to generation.

THE OTHER SIDE OF THE HILLS

The old man is so old that his face seems just as grey as his hair. His words are slow, and he does not work any more. Every day he sits with the children under the big old mango tree, telling stories of his young days. This is one of his stories.

'Our tribe has a tradition that a young man should leave his village and walk far on the other side of the hills before coming back to settle down.

When I was sixteen I went. My father was a rich man – he had two oxen. He was also a kind man, and gave me the smaller ox with the milk-white horns as a gift for my journey.

We left the village and walked over the plains until we reached the hills. I then rode the ox up over the hills to beyond. On the other side, at the foot of the hills, there was a wide flat place where many cattle were grazing. Among the cattle I was not pleased to see a large strong and fierce bull.

I was frightened, and wondered how I was going to get past this monster when the great magic happened: my ox spoke! "Wait on that rock while I fight the bull. I'll be back soon." I waited as I'd been told, and watched in wonder while my ox fought the fierce bull. Soon I could see nothing, as the battle was so furious that it threw up all the dust of the plain. Then there was a final fall, and silence. As the dust cleared my ox came limping back. The bull was dead.

Even though he looked sore my ox told me to climb onto his back. We crossed the plain heading for a distant kopje. When we reached this little rocky hill I felt hungry. My ox seemed to know my thoughts:
"Tap on my horn twice, then twice more." I did so, and at our feet appeared a heap of wonderful foods: fresh fish and ripe fruits, and

grass glistening with dew for the ox. When we had eaten our fill the ox told me to tap on the other horn. What was left of the food vanished. There was nothing wasted. Happy and full, we went to sleep.

The next day we crossed a desert. On the other side we met another herd of cattle which had an even larger, fiercer bull. My ox again commanded me to wait. "This time I will die. You must pick up my fallen horns when it is over." The fight was terrible – I heard it all, but again saw nothing through the dust. When it was over there was no sign of my ox but for

his horns lying beside the fallen bull.

Sadly I walked on, not really looking in what direction I was going. But I was lucky and by nightfall I had reached a village. Here, the people had had no water for a long time. The children could not remember the days when there had been water and a big crop of mealies. I wondered if my ox's magic was still in the horns. I tapped a horn, and suddenly the rock behind me split in two. A stream rushed into the village and flowed down into the valley to make a river. Then there was dancing and cries of joy. That night we all slept happy after a great party.

I left when the sun rose. By midday I was hungry and sat down to tap the horns. Nothing happened. Again I tapped, and again nothing happened. I was cross and even a little frightened because I had come to rely on the horns. Then I noticed that the horns were almost brown. My ox's horns were milk-white. My ox's horns had been stolen! I jumped to my feet, ran back along the river to the village and found the thief.

The thief begged my forgiveness, saying: "We were afraid that without the horns the water would stop. I am sorry. I should have trusted you after you were so generous." I felt sorry for him, so I tapped the horns and shared food with the village before continuing on my journey.

That night I was very tired and could see no dwellings, so this time the horns provided me with a hut as well as food. I fell into a deep sleep. In the morning I was woken up by laughter. Looking out I saw the most beautiful girl in the world with her sisters and friends going

out to their fields to work. I followed them and watched hidden behind a tree. Their crops were poor and withering, so I tapped the horns. What stunned amazement, then cries of joy when they realised what was all around them! Instead of thin hanging brown plants, the crops were now strong and green and heavy with produce. I laughed and came out from behind the tree.

Mapula, the beautiful one, and the other girls took me to their home. I spent many happy days in their village until I had gathered enough courage to ask for Mapula to be my wife.

Her father was sad when I asked his permission to take his daughter away. "I could not be more pleased, but I will be shamed. I have no lobola, no dowry, to give with her. I am a poor man. I have nothing to give as the traditional bridal gift." I said that he must not worry and that I would come back the next morning.

Before leaving my hut the next day I tapped the horns. Nothing appeared, but I had a feeling that everything was alright. I set off for Mapula's father's home. He came rushing out to greet me. "Look, look! I am rich! I can give you a splendid lobola with my daughter." He was leading an ox which he handed over to me. It was my ox! I looked to where the horns should have been hanging from my belt. They had gone. They were back on his head.

My ox provided the most magnificent feast in telling memory. For every one tub of beer made by the women, the ox made it two. After many days and nights of celebrating it was time for us to

go. Mapula and I got on the ox and set off for the return journey to my village.

We reached the final range of hills at night and sat down to eat meat roasted on our fire. Mapula and I then slept wrapped together in my blanket, full and happy. But in the morning the ox had disappeared. We could find no ox, no horns – no sign of him at all. I was sad because I knew now that my ox was now just a magic memory. We were home, back from the other side of the hills.'

Now, today, when the old man tells this story, Mapula his wife laughs with the children in amazement and disbelief. Of course Mapula knows the truth, because after all she comes from the other side of the hills.

African, Botswana

THE GREAT CHASE

Mirragen the Catman was a great fisherman. In fact he was the most famous fisherman on the West Coast. His fishing skills were known far and wide, and now he only went after fish that were big enough to test his skill. The only problem with this was that he had caught all the big fish that there were in the area where he lived.

'I'm off to look for some decent big fish,' he told his family. 'I'm fed up with all the tiny stuff here. I shall find and catch the biggest fish alive.' So saying, he set off on his search.

Mirragen followed a river for many days, but all the fish he saw were too small for his consideration. He wanted to find a fish that would really test his skill. He was tired of catching fish so easily.

At a bend, the river joined with another river. Here there was a large deep pool. Mirragen sat down and looked deep down into the water. To his joy he saw two huge eyes staring back up at him.

This pool was the home of a creature whose ancestors had lived here for many centuries. Gurangatch was half fish and half lizard. He had always lived in the same place, and so had grown amazingly huge. Mirragen knew the legends about Gurangatch, and so became excited at the thought of catching this powerful fish.

He summoned up his magic power, and casting spells he started to make Gurangatch rise towards the surface of the pool. Mirragen had, however, truly met his match, and his magic was not quite strong enough against Gurangatch's own powers. Exhausted, Mirragen had to give up for the time being. He prepared a bed for the night, and lay down to make plans for the next day's attack.

Meanwhile, down in the depths of the pool, Gurangatch was worried. He had never been so near death before. He too had heard of the legendary Mirragen.
'I can resist his magic, but he's sure

to use more than magic next time. What will he choose – a spear, a net?' Gurangatch tried to plan his defence, but got so tired thinking out all the possibilities that he fell asleep.

Suddenly he was floating up to the top again. Gurangatch awoke to find Mirragen using his magic again. This time there was also something else – a terrible taste and smell in the water. Mirragen had put bark poison in the pool! Gurangatch did not wait to think – he had to get away. Breaking out of the magic spell with a crash and splash of his huge tail, he leapt out of the pool and set off away from Mirragen the Catman.

Mirragen could not believe what he was seeing. In his haste to get away, Gurangatch was ploughing through earth and rock. The trail he left behind was filling up from the deep pool, and a third river was being formed. Mirragen rushed to follow the great monster. At least he would have an obvious trail.

Mirragen continued his pursuit of Gurangatch for several days. The new river twisted and wound around each outcrop of rocks that had halted his progress. Eventually Gurangatch had come to rocks which he could not get round, and so decided to burrow his way through them. This slowed him down and Mirragen was able to catch up.

Mirragen punched great holes in the rock down to where the fish was pushing through. He threw spears straight down, once or twice missing Gurangatch by only half a scale's width. But still the great fish got away.

Meanwhile the people who lived on the land were shouting out to Mirragen,
'Give it up! Gurangatch is breaking up the land. Look what has happened to our lives – where there were homes there is now a great river.' But instead of stopping to consider their troubles Mirragen asked for their help.
'Help me to trap the mighty fish, then we can feast on him together.'

The people were too afraid of Gurangatch's magic to help Mirragen. They were afraid that perhaps Gurangatch's power was greater than that of Mirragen. They just shook their heads and

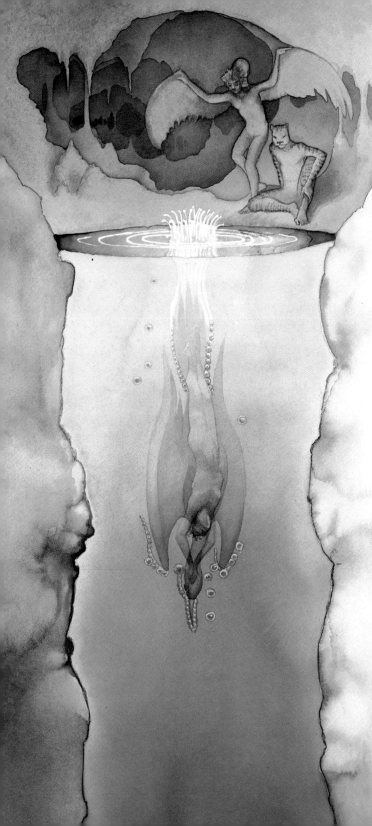

continued to mend their lives. One man only, feeling that he would like to give Mirragen some encouragement, said, 'Try the Birdmen. They might help – Gurangatch is going their way.'

Mirragen followed the newly formed river into the next valley where the Birdmen lived. Here, he found that two of the Birdmen, Diverman and the Duckman, were willing to help him. They had heard of the legendary power of the Catman, and were sure that together they would succeed in defeating the mighty fish.

The three followed Gurangatch through the underground maze of tunnels he was creating with his river. Finally they cornered him in a deep pool that he had carved out for himself. The Duckman went into the pool, and after a while brought out a large silver fish. Triumphant he threw it at Mirragen's feet.
'What's this rubbish! Gurangatch is no tiny creature like this!' Mirragen kicked the dead fish away in disgust.

Mirragen decided to go into the pool with Diverman, but Diverman had flown up into the air first to start his dive, and so could go down much further than the Catman. Mirragen waited a long time before Diverman finally came back with a piece of fish flesh. 'You will never catch him, Mirragen. I only managed to tear off this piece of flesh.'

In a way Mirragen was pleased. He had a piece of Gurangatch to eat, which was more than any other man had been able to do. And he still had a great enemy to chase whenever he felt bored with other fish. He thanked Diverman and Duckman for their help and set off on the long journey home with the piece of Gurangatch tied to his spear. It shone in the dying sunlight.

Now if you go to the West Coast you can still see great rivers with caves and deep holes that mark the way of Mirragen the Catman's journey in pursuit of the monster Gurangatch.

Aboriginal

SCATTER THROUGHOUT THE LAND

Waqiyasma the chief heard the fearful noise and came out of his dwelling to see what was happening. The whole village seemed to be fighting each other! This was terrible. The Pai people were not warriors, but were peaceful people who grew crops and gathered plants for food, medicine, and for weaving. How had this fighting started?

Waqiyasma the chief climbed up onto a rock and shouted out in a voice that could be heard all round Meriwhitica Canyon, and probably could be heard all round the Lower Grand Canyon itself. 'Stop fighting! We are Pai. We are a peaceful people. I am calling a council to find out what started this terrible fighting.'

It had all started with an accident. The children had been playing with mud balls. One boy had not noticed that some of the balls he had in his pile had been left over from the last game. Those were harder than the new ones. He threw, and hit his friend by mistake. Out of surprise more than pain, the friend cried out. The other children thought that the first boy had done it all deliberately, and so they too started throwing the old, hard mud balls at him.

The boy was frightened, so he and a few of his closest friends who did not accuse him made new mud balls to throw back in defence. This time, though, they put stones in the balls. These really did hurt, and soon there were cuts and blood too. Some of the children ran crying to their parents. The parents seeing the cuts and blood were angry, and joined the fight. Soon the whole village was fighting and making the terrible noise that Waqiyasma heard.

Waqiyasma was very sad. As chief he was responsible for his people. In future it would be seen that it was his fault that the peaceful Pai had fought amongst themselves while he was chief. He knew what must be done:

'You must all leave this place. You are no longer one peaceful people. You must all scatter throughout the land.'

The people were also sad at

what had happened, but they knew that their chief was right. They could never go back to how they had been before the fight. They must leave their Indian Garden in Meriwhitica Canyon and each find a different place to live.

The Pai people asked wise Waqiyasma to lead them. When they were ready, they all gathered by the pool at the rim of the canyon. They drank the water, and filled their skin pouches. Then they set off.

They named each place as they went: Pipe Hill, North Tank, Milkweed Canyon. They stayed in each of these places for a few days and nights, because they had to try out each area before deciding whether they would like to live there.

The journey continued past Bee Hill to Peach Springs Canyon, then on to Cataract Canyon. Here, a large group decided they preferred Peach Springs and so they turned back to settle there. These were called the Hualupai people, who live there still. Waqiyasma and the others continued to the south.

Those that stayed at White River were called the Apaches. Those that settled at Salt Spring were called the Hopi. Later some of the Hopi went even further south, and this new group were called the Navajo.

Waqiyasma continued to lead

what was left of the Pai down through Coyote Springs and past Grand Wash Cliffs. A short distance from the place they called Hackberry they saw a deer. It was shot and eaten, and the people who stayed here became great hunters.

Further on Waqiyasma dropped seeds on the ground, and while they were camping there the shoots started growing. The people who stayed there became great farmers.

Waqiyasma took the remaining Pai along the Sandy River until they reached hot springs. There he took a lame boy who was exhausted from the long journey, and put him into the hot water. After a few days the boy felt so well that his family group decided to stay. Waqiyasma said to them: 'Many people will travel to this place for cures. You people will be known for your medicines and for your kindness.'

Nearly all the groups had found new places to live. Those that were left were called the Yavapais, and they went off towards the east. Waqiyasma was now old and sick, so he let them continue on their own. He returned to the Indian Garden in Meriwhitica Canyon to die.

Now all the Pai people were scattered, and they were becoming different tribes speaking their own different languages. Some were hunters, some farmers, and some healers. Some lived in the hills, some by the rivers, and some on the plains. But never again were any of the people as peaceful as the original Pai had been.

Waqiyasma died in the cave in Meriwhitica Canyon. He left instructions that his body should not be taken away to be burned. He must be left in the cave so that there would be a memory of the origin of the people that had divided and scattered throughout the land.

North American Indian, Hualupai

THE ROAD OF DEATH

Some roads have a reputation for being dangerous. Some have steep drops and some have blind corners. This road had a reputation for being so dangerous that it was called the Road of Death. Everyone who travelled on this road died. If they started at one end they never reached the other.

At one end of this road there was a village where there lived an old wise man. This man knew many things, but one thing still made him curious. He wanted to know what happened to people on the Road of Death.

One day he decided that he would travel on this road. He was very old, and near enough to death anyway. He had had a good life and was ready to die if that was necessary. He took one precaution though: he disguised himself as a bullock.

When people die the chain of life is cut. This chain is usually invisible, so you can never tell when it is being broken. The old man wanted to be able to see what was happening to his chain, so by turning himself into a bullock he would have the chain hanging round his neck in full view.

The old man-bullock set off along the road. Nothing happened

for the first few hours, and as he was tired he paused under a shady tree. While resting he saw a long fat poisonous snake of a kind that he had never seen before. The snake seemed to be going in the same direction as he was, so the old man-bullock decided to follow it.

First the snake went into a shelter which was a travellers' rest. There it slid about quietly at night killing everyone while they were asleep.

The next day the snake went on to where the road crossed a deep river with a terrible current. On the

bank stood a few people wondering how they were going to cross. The old man-bullock was amazed to see the snake change into a bullock just like himself. The only difference was that the snake-bullock did not have a chain round its neck.

The snake-bullock went up to the people. One of them said to the others, 'Look, there is a bullock. It looks strong enough to take us across the river. Let's climb onto its back.' They all climbed on, and were pleased that they had been so lucky to find such an easy way of crossing. But where the river was

at its deepest and fastest, and where there was no hope of reaching either bank, the snake-bullock turned back into a snake and swam away. All the people were drowned. But still the old man-bullock followed this terrible snake. The snake killed more travellers on the road who were journeying on their own. It also killed any animals that crossed its path.

The most amazing thing the old man-bullock saw was when the snake changed itself into a maiden. The snake-maiden sat crying on a rock when she saw two young men passing by. She explained to them that her mother and father had just drowned in the river. She was now all alone in the world, and did not know what to do.

The taller of the young men, who was also the elder, said that he would take her home and look after her as his wife. She looked up at him and smiled gratefully. 'Would you do me a favour before we set off?' she asked. 'Please bring me a cup of water to drink from that well.' He went off willingly,

feeling pleased that he had found such a beautiful young wife.

When he returned, she thanked him and said, 'I think you ought to know that while you were away your friend told me to run away with him and leave you behind.'
'That is a lie!' shouted the second young man.
'Are you calling my wife a liar, you thief?' The two men fell upon each other fighting with their fists. Then the snake-maiden put rocks near the fighting men, and soon they had picked them up to hit each other. As the sun went down that day the two young men lay dead by the side of the well. The snake-maiden took another drink from the cup, and then turned back into a snake.

The old man-bullock followed the snake as it slid away, but in the dark he lost the trail. He could not see any sign of the snake anywhere. When he decided to give up looking for the night, he saw an old man on the road in front of him. 'Can I help you, old bullock?' the old man asked. The old man-bullock was about to ask whether he had seen a long fat snake pass

this way, when he suddenly realised that the old man in front of him was himself! The old man reached out to catch the man-bullock's chain and laughed.
'What a piece of luck to find a bullock wandering with no master, and with a chain all ready to lead him home.' But before the chain could be touched the old man-bullock turned and galloped home.

He had almost reached his village when he saw the snake-man in front of him.
'You are a wise old man,' the snake-man said. 'But even with your wisdom, one day I will get you. I have left you alone this time because you are not ready to die. I only take those that are ready. We will not meet again for many years.'

Suddenly the old man found himself back at home, sitting in the shade of the big old tree where he always went when he wanted to think. Had he dreamed his journey along the Road of Death?

Indian

A VISIT TO THE SPIRITS OF MOUNT KATAHDIN

Once a young brave went out to hunt. He wanted to be alone, so he followed the river Penobscot all the way to the foot of Mount Katahdin. There he set up a camp and started to hunt. For several days he saw no-one, nor saw or heard any signs of people. His hunting was good, so he was happy.

One day when he was searching the snow for signs of animals that had passed, he saw the clear outlines of snow-shoes. He returned to his camp so that he would not meet the person that was walking about.

The next day, the same thing happened again. This time he set off on a different path, and yet still found fresh snow-shoe tracks. This happened every day after that. The young hunter was puzzled. Every day, in whatever direction he chose to walk, he would find these tracks. But all this time he never saw or heard anyone.

The hunter had become so curious now that he decided to find out who was making these tracks. So this time when he came across the marks made by the snow-shoes he did not return to his camp. He

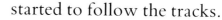

started to follow the tracks.

The tracks led up Mount Katahdin. The walking was easy at first, but soon became more difficult as more and more rocks appeared. The hunter was beginning to think that perhaps this was not such a good idea when the snow-shoe tracks reached what looked like a path. So many snow-shoes had walked in this direction that a flat and hard path had been made in the snow. It was now easier for the hunter to take off his own snow-shoes to continue. There was still no sign of any people.

Soon the path came to an end facing a high outcrop of rock. Again the hunter was puzzled because the tracks seemed to continue right up to the rock face. He looked up to see how high the rock was – perhaps the people had climbed over it, he thought – when he was amazed to see a beautiful tall maiden standing on a ledge just above his head!

He did not speak, but stood there with his mouth open. The maiden did not speak either, but seemed to be able to put thoughts into his head. The hunter started to walk forward into the rock. Half his mind told him that he was mad to be walking into hard rock. The other half told him that everything was alright, because the maiden was there.

The rock seemed to melt into thin air as the young man walked forward. The maiden was now in front of him, leading him with her smile. In what must have been the very centre of the mountain they reached a large cavern with a round flat floor and a pointed cone for a ceiling. In the middle of the floor sat an old grey man. He looked as if he had been carved out of rock. His eyebrows looked like great slabs of stone, and his cheeks were long and craggy.

No-one spoke, but again the hunter found his head was full of

their thoughts. He knew that he had been chosen to come here to learn something of the great truths of the world. In his hunting he had always treated Nature with respect. He never took more game than he needed, and he always tried to cause as little pain to animals as possible. Now Nature was rewarding him with knowledge.

As soon as the hunter realised this great honour, he heard terrible noises. Crashes and roars seemed to be coming from all around the cavern. Then from the far side of the round floor he saw two youths approaching. They were the brothers of the smiling sunny maiden. The youths were tall and powerful, and they too had eyebrows of stone.

The noises continued as the youths got nearer to the hunter. His head then told him that they were Thunder and Lightning. Their father, the old man of rock, sent out the two brothers from time to time to keep an eye on the people who lived on and around Mount Katahdin. Lightning was to strike down those who were doing wrong, while Thunder was to growl a warning to all the others.

After the old man of rock had put his knowledge into the hunter's head, the maiden led him back to the rock face. He found himself gazing up to the sunny blue sky at the top of the tall sheer face of rock. At his feet was deep snow, so he put on his snow-shoes to return to his camp. There was no longer a flattened path, and the original snow-shoe tracks which he had followed before had disappeared. All that was left in the snow was a trail marked by his own snow-shoes. Following this trail he reached his camp and his store of game.

The hunter was excited with his new knowledge. Gathering up everything he set off for home. When he arrived back at his village he found that he had been missing for seven years! The whole village celebrated his return. He was now no longer a young man, so he was made an elder of the village. He was respected for his journey of discovery which had added to the knowledge of his people.

North American Indian, Algonquin

ESCAPE FROM FINN

The great warrior Finn MacCool was sad and lonely because his wife had just died. When he told his friends about his loneliness they advised him to ask to marry Grania, the daughter of Cormac the High King of Ireland. Cormac agreed with pleasure, and arranged for a great feast to take place.

Finn came to the feast with all his warriors. Finn sat at the high table with the King and Queen and Grania, while the court and all the warriors sat at tables set out in a horseshoe shape facing them. At the beginning of the meal Grania asked her mother what the feast was for.

'To announce your betrothal to Finn, my dear,' her mother answered.

'Am I to marry that old man! He is older than my father.'

'He is Finn MacCool, the great warrior, my dear. He will make a good husband.'

Grania said nothing more and continued eating and drinking. After a while she turned to Finn and asked him to tell her who all his warriors were. He was pleased to describe them and their skills and qualities one by one. Grania was really only interested in one of the warriors, and listened closely when Finn described him.

'The warrior with the black curly hair and the smiling grey eyes is Dermot of the Shining Face. He is the most chivalrous and generous of all my warriors. And next to him . . .' But Grania was not listening any more. She was thinking about her plan.

The feasting was now very

noisy, and everyone was half drunk. Grania beckoned to her servant. She told the girl to bring the giant silver goblet that held enough for seven giants to drink. Grania took out of her sleeve a pouch with magic powder. She put this into the goblet which she then filled with wine. Grania then handed the goblet to Finn.

'This is for you to drink – a gift from me.' Finn took the goblet and drank half the wine. Then he passed it on to the King and the Queen, and all the others of high rank that were near him. Soon the goblet was empty, and all those who had drunk the wine were fast asleep!

Grania ran to Dermot and begged him to take her away.

'I cannot take you from your father, and from Finn who is to marry you,' answered Dermot. Grania remembered that Finn had said that Dermot was the most chivalrous of his warriors.

'I beg you as a maiden in distress. I need help to escape from a marriage which I do not want. Are you not sworn to help all women in trouble?'

Dermot did not know what he should do. He was indeed sworn to defend all women in distress, but he was also sworn in loyalty to Finn MacCool. Dermot asked his fellow warriors what he should do. They said that the greater bond was to Grania. So Dermot put on his swords and daggers, said goodbye to his fellow warriors, and left immediately with Grania. He knew that the next time he saw any of his friends he would have to kill them. They were Finn's warriors, and Finn would chase him until one of them was dead.

For many days and nights Dermot and Grania fled through the glens and forests of Ireland. They dared not stop and ate berries for food as they went. One day, though, Dermot could see that Grania was too tired to continue much further. They stopped in a wood, and Dermot used the young trees around them to build a shelter. The shelter had a large space in the centre, and seven doors facing out in all directions. Grania felt safe for a while but Dermot knew that Finn could not be far away.

Sure enough Finn found the shelter, and surrounded it with his warriors. Grania was distressed because she knew that she was too tired to run any further. She cried out in anger and frustration. Angus of the Birds, the god of Love and Beauty, heard her cry, and taking pity on her appeared in the shelter. 'Come into my cloak and I will take you away unseen,' he said.

Dermot agreed that Grania should go with Angus, but he must stay and face Finn and the warriors.

When Grania was safely away, Dermot asked at each door who was defending it. He did not want to kill any of his friends. His fight should be with Finn himself.

Finn was at the fifth door. Dermot said, 'Finn, this is the door that I shall come out of.' When he heard this Finn made ready to fight Dermot. But Dermot did not come through the door: he took a young

sapling and used it as a pole to help him jump high over the door. Before Finn and the warriors had realised what had happened Dermot had made his escape and was already far away.

Dermot found Angus of the Birds and Grania in a secret place. They were having a fine meal of

roast boar, and he was pleased to rest and eat after all this time on the run. When they had eaten and slept, Angus gave them some advice, 'When you are running away from Finn never climb up into a tree with only one trunk, never go into a cave with only one entrance, never go onto an island with only one bay, never cook your food where you have hunted, never eat your food where you have cooked, never sleep where you have eaten, and never sleep in the same place twice.' Angus then left.

Grania and Dermot continued to flee from Finn for many months, until they reached a forest in the west of the country. In this forest was a magic tree. This tree was the home of the horrible giant Sharvan. Finn and his warriors would not want to fight the giant, and so Dermot thought they would be safe there.

Dermot went to get permission from Sharvan to stay in the forest. Sharvan said that he would let them stay so long as Dermot and Grania did not come near his tree or pick its berries.

Dermot agreed. Dermot and Grania were pleased to be able to rest for a while after all this running.

Finn came to the forest, but did not want to go in himself. Luckily he found two young men who wanted to join his warriors. 'You have to pass a test first,' he told them. 'You must bring me berries from the magic tree in that forest. You must kill the giant who is guarding the tree.' He did not tell the young men that the giant was so frightful that even he, the great Finn, would not go near him.

The young men went into the forest and met Dermot. They told Dermot of their task. Grania heard, and asked what was so special about the berries.
'They are fairy berries and they give great liveliness to those who eat them,' said Dermot.
'In that case I want some,' said Grania. 'The young men can bring some back for me too.'

Dermot could not let the young men go to their death without trying to help, so he set off with them to see the giant. The

giant had made a bargain with Dermot, and so did not expect to have to fight him. Dermot told Sharvan that he had come for berries. Sharvan reached for his club, but too late. Dermot was too quick for him, he grabbed the club and brought it down on the giant's head. Shavan was dead.

When Finn saw the young men returning with the berries he knew that Dermot had killed the giant. Then Finn's grandson Oscar said, 'O Finn, can you not see that Dermot is no real enemy. He is an honourable man, who will not even see your servants die needlessly. If you do not forgive him I will join him and be your enemy forever.'

After thinking about it a long time, Finn forgave Dermot. Cormac the High King of Ireland also pardoned Dermot, so Grania and Dermot went to live on their own land in Kerry, where they brought up a family of five fine children.

Irish

JOURNEY THROUGH HELL TO HEAVEN AND BACK

Miao Shan had defied her father. The king wanted his daughter Miao Shan to marry, but Miao Shan was determined to become a nun. She wanted to devote her life to seeking perfection through her prayers.

The king could not allow himself to appear to be weak, so when someone disobeyed him – even if that someone was his daughter – he had to order an execution. The queen pleaded with the king to save Miao Shan's life, and asked him to cancel the execution. The king asked Miao Shan to change her mind, but Miao Shan just repeated quietly that, although she had no wish to disobey her father, she still felt that she would become a better person by devoting her life to thinking about God and to leading a religious life.

The king was furious that his daughter was so disobedient, and ordered the execution to take place the very next day. The Pearly Emperor, ruler of the First Heaven, heard of this and summoned one of his servants.
'Whatever knife or sword is used tomorrow to execute Miao Shan will break before it touches her. In this way nothing will spoil her. I will see that she suffers no pain. When she dies, you will immediately become a tiger, and will carry her body to the pine wood. There, you will put this potion in her mouth, so that her body will always remain young. Now go.'

The next morning all was set for the execution to begin. The sword was raised over Miao Shan's head, but as soon as it was brought down it broke. This happened with all the swords they tried. At last the executioner had to use a rope of silk to carry out his orders.

As soon as Miao Shan was dead, a huge tiger leapt through the crowd of soldiers. He lifted the body onto his back and ran away towards the pine wood. The soldiers rushed to tell the king, but all he said was, 'At least she is dead. My orders have been carried out.'

Miao Shan's soul had risen onto a golden cloud as soon as her body died. While her body was being carried off to the pine wood by the tiger-servant, her soul was

beginning the journey to hell. She looked round and saw that the whole place was bleak. Nothing was alive at all: nothing to see, nothing to hear, nothing at all.

She was feeling miserable as she walked on her journey, when suddenly a blue glow appeared in front of her. There stood a young man.

'I am the servant of Yen Wang, the Lord of Hell. I'm to lead you to the infernal regions.' Puzzled, but

trusting, Miao Shan followed the young man. He was so far ahead that all she could see to follow was a blue glow through the nothingness.

There are ten infernal regions, and Miao Shan went through them all. All contained nothing, and strangely some seemed even emptier than others. Miao Shan said nothing, but calmly followed the blue glow. When she had gone through all the infernal regions, she reached a place where the Gods of the Ten Hells were gathered to meet her.

The ten gods had been very impressed with all that they had heard about the king's disobedient daughter.

'Tell us,' they asked. 'Is it true that when you say your prayers that you can make evil disappear? Show us – we want to see and hear if it is true.'

'I will say my prayers only if you bring everyone who is kept in the ten hells to hear me.' The gods agreed. The inhabitants of all ten hells were brought before Miao Shan and the Gods of the Ten Hells.

Miao Shan began to say her prayers. As she spoke, the nothingness melted into the shape of heaven: there were beautiful hills and valleys full of sweet-smelling blossoms as far as the eye could see. The Pearly Emperor had known that Miao Shan was full of goodness. Near where she stood now there was a pine wood with a tiger standing next to a body. It was her body, and her soul now floated back into it.

Miao Shan had been too good for hell. She had turned hell into heaven with her prayers. This did not please P'an Kuan who was the keeper of the Book of the Living and the Dead. He complained to the Pearly Emperor that, if there was still to be good and bad, there must be a separate heaven and hell. Now that Miao Shan had made the two the same – what was to be done?

The Pearly Emperor decided that the best thing to do was to put Miao Shan back onto earth. Then the Ten Hells could go back to how it had been before, except for all the people that Miao Shan had saved.

Back among the living again, but no longer the daughter of the king, Miao Shan was able to go up into a lonely place in the mountains, where she could devote herself to seeking perfection in her prayers.

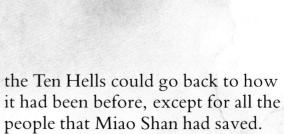

Chinese

THE CITY OF ULTIMATE BEAUTY AND HAPPINESS

Aziz was a very rich merchant who loved giving parties. He was a happy man who liked having lots of fun with all his friends. Each week he would give at least one large afternoon feast in the shade of his cool covered courtyard round a pool of lovely water lilies.

Everyone always enjoyed these parties, so Aziz was amazed to see a stranger crying there one afternoon. He went over to the man, and asked him what was wrong. The stranger stayed silent, but Aziz insisted on knowing what was the matter.

'I will tell you, as you are so insistant. I decided one day to journey to a region in northern India. I was a well respected merchant, and so many others joined my caravan. We were almost there, with only one more day's journey to go when a terrible storm arose. We tried to stay close to each other, but when the next morning brought a calm sky I was alone. I had lost my companions.

For days I wandered round looking for the rest of my caravan, and trying to reach one of the towns I knew should be close. But I just kept going round in circles in the desert.

One night I thought I was about to be attacked when a young man found me, and told me of his home. He was the gatekeeper of the most beautiful city: the city of ultimate happiness and beauty. I followed him to his home . . .'

At this point in the story two cats who had been fighting on the roof of Aziz's covered courtyard rolled off the roof into the pool. They fled, wet and hissing, through the guests, who had been listening intently to the stranger. In the confusion the stranger disappeared.

Aziz ordered his servants to go out and search for the stranger. He met every caravan that was passing and made inquiries. Days, then weeks, then months passed and still Aziz did not know who the man was, where he had come from, or where he had disappeared to. Aziz was obsessed with the story of the city of happiness. He must find this wonderful place.

So Aziz gathered a fine caravan to travel to the region in northern India. There he hoped to follow the stranger's trail. Aziz spent such a long time wandering in the desert, finding nothing, that slowly he lost all his friends, and even all his servants. After a year of searching he was alone.

Terrible storms would come up overnight, and Aziz would hide in his cloak. During the day trees, or people, or lakes would form and hover on the horizon, then the mirages would vanish. Aziz saw no-one – not even a thief, until one particularly stormy night.

Almost frozen by the biting wind, Aziz suddenly felt a hand upon his shoulder. A tall young man was looking down at him. 'Are you the gatekeeper?' Aziz shouted through the wind. The young man did not reply but asked, 'Where are you going? What are you doing alone in the desert for so many days?' Aziz told him of the stranger's story, and of his search for the city of happiness and beauty.

'There is no such place. You are searching for nowhere. Come with me and I will show you the way home.' But Aziz refused. He was determined to find the end to the stranger's story.

'If you are determined to ruin yourself with this wandering, then take this dagger. When you are exhausted – and only then – take it out and hold it in front of you. Then when you have regained your strength, put it back in its scabbard.' With these words the young man handed over a silver dagger in an intricately carved ivory and gold scabbard, and disappeared.

The storm was gone, and Aziz set off with more hope than he had had for several days. He walked all day and all night for a week without stopping. Then, when he was about to fall down from exhaustion, Aziz took out the dagger. The blade twinkled in the strong sunlight, and Aziz blinked. Beyond the dagger he could see the most marvellous city with walls of shining white and roofs of gold. Holding the dagger out in front of

him, Aziz now ran towards the city. He forgot his tiredness, and rushed on not looking where he was running. He tripped and fell, dropping the dagger into a deep pool which had appeared in front of him.

Aziz did not mind about the dagger – after all, he had found the city. But when he looked up all he could see was a poor farmhouse.

The farmer had seen Aziz, who had collapsed, and he took in the exhausted merchant. Aziz was so tired that he slept for several days in the farmer's loft. Early one morning Aziz heard the farmer going about his work in the yard below. Aziz looked out of the small window and saw the farmer walking across his field to a strange tree. The tree had a ring of mist round it, but in the middle a wide beam came down from the sun to light up the shining pale leaves. As the farmer approached the tree a slim white hand appeared from the tree to take the cup of wine he offered. Then the wine, the hand, the beam and the mist all disappeared, and the farmer returned to the house.

Aziz watched this happen every day. After seven days he came down from the loft and crept along behind the farmer on his visit to the tree. Just as the hand came down Aziz leapt forward and pulled it hard.

Everything went dark. Aziz was pulled up through speeding darkness, until he found himself wrapped tight in what seemed like a small bag or sack. He tried to tear himself free and, while he was rolling this way and that, he hit a wooden door.

The door was part of a great gateway, and now the gatekeeper opened the door. He opened the strange sack and let Aziz out. The

were made of gold, the streets were made of marble, there were flowers everywhere, multicoloured birds ate fat ripe fruits – this must be the city he was looking for.

Aziz was taken into a palace where the furniture was made of ebony and agate. He was led to a throne, where he had robes of finest cotton and silk put on him. He could not believe that this was happening: he was the king of the city of ultimate beauty and happiness. He ordered fruit and wine for everyone – he ordered a party with music and dancing. He was so happy he danced and sang until it was quite dark, then he danced and sang through the night. He forgot his tiredness and the years of wandering through the desert. He could never be happier than he was at this moment.

Aziz noticed the reflections of the gold roofs in the lily ponds. It was dawn. The gatekeeper came to greet Aziz, and took him by the hand. Aziz did not realise what was happening until he reached the great wooden door. In a blink he was outside with the sack wrapped

young man led Aziz through the doorway, and Aziz looked round him in amazement. The door had been inlaid with rubies, the gates

round his shoulders where the cotton and silk had been.

Aziz banged and banged on the door, shouting to be let back in. The door opened, and there stood his old servant. What joy, what rejoicing there was now that Aziz had found his way back to his old home. Everyone was happy to see him again. He was thin and tired – obviously what he needed was a party!

While everyone else was celebrating his return, Aziz sat quietly in his covered courtyard and cried. He now knew the end of the story: you can only visit the city of ultimate happiness and beauty once, and on that one day you will be king.

Persian